Heredities

WINNER OF THE WALT WHITMAN AWARD FOR 2009

Sponsored by the Academy of American Poets, the Walt Whitman Award is given annually to the winner of an open competition among American poets who have not yet published a book of poems.

JUDGE FOR 2009: Juan Felipe Herrera

heredities

POEMS

J. MICHAEL MARTINEZ

Louisiana State University Press

Baton Rouge

Published by Louisiana State University Press
Copyright © 2010 by J. Michael Martinez
All rights reserved
Manufactured in the United States of America
LSU Press Paperback Original
First printing

DESIGNER: Michelle A. Neustrom
TYPEFACE: Adobe Garamond Pro
PRINTER AND BINDER: Thomson-Shore, Inc.

LIBRARY OF CONGRESS CATALOGING-IN-PUBLICATION DATA
Martinez, J. Michael, 1978–
    Heredities : poems / J. Michael Martinez.
      p. cm.
    ISBN 978-0-8071-3643-0 (pbk. : alk. paper)
    I. Title.
    PS3613.A78644H47 2010
    811'.6—dc22

                                    2009047071

The paper in this book meets the guidelines for permanence and durability of the Committee on
Production Guidelines for Book Longevity of the Council on Library Resources. ∞

The author is deeply grateful to the editors of the following journals in which earlier versions of
some of these poems appeared: *New American Writing, The Colorado Review, Five Fingers Review,
Crab Orchard Review, The Bitter Oleander, Practice: New Writing + Art, Word for/Word, Copper Nickel,
Eleven Eleven,* and *Parthenon West.*

I also extend much gratitude to *Five Fingers Review* for the *Five Fingers Review* Poetry Prize.

"In the Year of the Jubilee" appeared as part of exhibits in collaboration with printmaker Britta
Ambauen at the University of Colorado at Boulder Art Museum in the spring of 2007 and in the
Westmont College Print Collection in the Reynolds Gallery, Santa Barbara, California, in the fall
of 2007.

Great thanks to my teachers Jennifer Atkinson, Eric Pankey, Susan Tichy, and Peggy Yocom for their
guidance and close friendship. Further gratitude to James Belflower, Brian Brodeur, Danielle Deulen,
Gabe Gomez, Katie Morris, Allegra Morton, Heather Pollock, John-Michael Rivera, Rebecca Stod-
dard, Chris Tanseer, Matt Thomas, and Elizabeth Winder for their advice, encouragement, and
friendship. Thanks also to George Mason University's MFA program for the financial support and
its outstanding creative community. Great thanks to LSU Press and their wonderful staff for making
this book a reality.

I am also deeply grateful to the late Reginald Shepherd for his compassionate and thoughtful
readings of these poems.

To Juan Felipe Herrera for selecting the work, my enduring and humble thanks.

for
The Martinez Family

Once the historical moment is gone the structure of feeling begins to fragment.

—JOHN STOREY, "The Analysis of Culture"

Our name shelters a stranger, about whom we know nothing
except that he is we ourselves.

—OCTAVIO PAZ

Contents

Heredities

Margin is the whiteness in our silence. I said, Difference is already spread between the body and the gaze. You said, We lament the name we give; we give word to find respite from the shallows between. Your irises close, black flowers folding toward the silence of their beginning. I place a cup of coffee before you. I said, The noun never sutures to the named body.

I

Heredities (1) *Etymology*

When she was seven, my grandmother suffered from fever and swollen glands. The doctors believed her tonsils were inflamed, that she needed surgery. Instead, she went to a curandera. The curandera divined that a jealous relative had cast a curse on her and, now, her language of kindness was bound to her throat, the unspoken swelling her glands.

As a child my grandmother spoke to santitos with a voice like a chestnut: ruddy and warm, seeds dropping from her mouth. The santitos would take her words into themselves, her voice growing within them like grapevines.

During the tonsillitis, when the words no longer fell like seeds from her lips, the santito's vineyards of accent and voice grew vapid, dry as a parched mouth. They went to her tongue and asked why silence imprisoned the words of the child, why lumps were present under her chin, why tears drew channels down her cheeks.

I asked my grandmother how her tongue replied. After touching my cheek, she told me she had a dream that night: She was within her lungs and she rose like breath through the moist of her throat. She remembered her tonsils swinging before her like fleshy apples, then a hand taking them into a fist, harvesting their sound. She told me her throat opened in two spots like insect eyes and the names of her children came flying through her wounds like peacocks.

Patting my thigh, she said, "That is why the name of your mother is *Maria,* because she is a prayer, a song of praise to the Holy Mother." She told me this, then showed me two scars on her throat—tiny scars, like two eyelids stitched closed.

Xicano

as light
        shaped by trajectory.

a wind settles in the body.
Echécatl the breath, the flint & spark.
the house of prayers.

I am

when sounds exchange questions
when light enters the lung
when given

the noun: a variable absence
a law   pinned to a quail's wing.

Maria

Mar
The   I
     Mother

a holy silence between
Self
            and the Marred
             Mary

               virgin verging in matrimony

   confess the blessed fruit
           uterus to vulva   round the belly

   A mari-
         gold mariolatry

   I doll of petals,
         stem and grace

        Chant *a murie*   the edge of lament

         the water of syllables

         exposes the rose

         beneath the noun

       Are you married to your name
          Mother?

        Even in Marriage
        the I is
            after erasure
        the Age at the end

when the   mare he
has ridden has rid
                the name

He Name Me Miklo

Miklo [meek-ló] slang *n.* 1. a Hispanic with light skin
2. Insult to dark-skinned Hispanics

My given name is _____
He who is like God

Son of God

      He name me Miklo
            because I am white-
                  r than his-
                      panics
Are then Hispanics
      of his-
            panic of culture
                no culture
no name
      no word
         non word

because I am no one
Miklo?

White

as the meat
within the shell

as the shell before the caw

a bleached weed
a fig
dusted to sweet the skin

egg albumen of peacock
butterfly

held to the ivory of oxen hoof
pulling
the space

between sins   I am

as I am so

the host   on the tongue
God of Bread

complexion of conquest
the salt of Lot

as God is
a crown of thorn
diadem of wheat

so am I the echo
calling fossil back to name

amaranth ash   spread across the light

Aporia

[1] *The Signified Seeks the Body*

I said, The Chicano shapes identity like an icicle fingering down from
the roof's edge. Pushing the hair back from your face, you said, Yes,
translucence freezes about its own boundaries, declaring the noun from the
water. I said, The name seeks to root in the arterial cavity; the tendons turn
from the blood like foreshadowing.

[2] *The Body Is Not Identical to the Self*

Like foreshadowing, I said, I inherit the absence of my language. You said, Spanish is drying blood. I said, Embellished language is for the poet who seeks to forget. Yes, you said, the moment identity is given the self is erased; a leaf breaks from its branch. I pour sugar on the table. The light pools in your eye, drowning adjectives in verbs.

[3] *The Mirror Image Is the Self of the Visible World*

Drowning adjectives in verbs, I said, flee through freezing, folded, untangling red. I said, I burned the skin to possess the self in human hope. You said, Origins complete themselves in one another. I said, Origin: the rattling of a mirror not quite firmly fastened to the image of the person before it. You placed the word "margin" in whiteness on the table between us.

[4] *The Word Is the Gaze between the Body and Its Listening*

Margin is the whiteness in our silence. I said, Difference is already spread between the body and the gaze. You said, We lament the name we give; we give word to find respite from the shallows between. Your irises close, black flowers folding toward the silence of their beginning. I place a cup of coffee before you. I said, The noun never sutures to the named body.

[5] *The Signifier Is Arbitrary*

I said, The noun never sutures to the named body. You said, Martinez is not your name, it is the cavity around which meaning defers. I said, My name is the absence between body and gaze. You said, You are the unclaimed syllogism. I said, I saw a child step from a curb and fall.

[6] *To Possess Identity, Difference Must Be Gathered*

I said, I step from a curb and fall. Toward the tension between your body
and its name, you said. I said, I am Mexican, next I can be a Chicano, she
with the hole at the end of identity. You said, Bless the throat drinking the
self, the swallow necessary for completion. I traced the scars on the table's
wood surface. I said, My culture swallows itself, an infinity without origin.

[7] *History Gathers in the Name We Never Are*

You said, An infinity with origin is the speech you foster. I said, I don't
speak Spanish, I am Hispanic. You said, Pan hisses in the center, the Gods
rise like bread from the noun; our syntax is the bond to the divinity we are.
I said, Sin taxes the soul, the name; our grammar is a construct of guilt.
You said, Teach the children to read the sin. I pick up my coat, empty the
pockets of lint, pennies. Icicles finger down from the roof's edge.

II

Heredities (2) *Corporeity*

Brash and handsome, my great-great-grandfather Francisco Beltran, the youngest of five brothers, often crossed himself with other women. He would play poker into the night with the rancheros, satisfying his want with what woman made herself available in those hours of chance.

The last, found beside a river, was washing her huipiles in the wet stillness. The olive-skinned woman wound the material taut, dipping them into the water, spiraling eddies across the surface. My great-great-grandmother Maria de Jesus, a Mexica married to the unfaithful Spaniard, came up from behind, uncoiling concentric circles as her hand calmly divided the current.

A ranchero later found the woman amongst her wash, unconscious. She grew feverish over the following hours, cotton sheets stained bloody; her skin softened into clay pallor as she died on the goose-feather mattress belonging to my rebisabuelo. A partera, the nearest healer, despite her massaging and prayers, could do nothing to revive her.

As soon as the pale one was at peace, the partera pulled the bloody sheets from the body. She spooned her hand between the woman's slick thighs. When her fingers tentatively parted the still warm lips, the partera found that space dammed with smooth river stones.

Water Poppies Open as the Mouth
The Body as Nature, History

> All motivations intermingle at the core of history, the internal
> becomes external . . . all as parts of the body.
> —MAURICE MERLEAU-PONTY

i.   *the positing of space, corporeal history*

medium of my body

bent to narrow rivers,

           touching of the touch
                  commits

totem to shape:

          jasmine buds,

     water poppies   open as the mouth.

               Propolis and juniper oil

   resinous viscera
   embowered in trees,

   life wholly aware of itself
   unbound and unsealed.

ii. into the language of seeing

eyes gather seed—

      perception as hive
      a bud of gold, a gold of blood

      apportioned in time

four wings fastened   by a row of resolutions

      reeved through revelation,

      place-world awoken,
      obscurity bonded to light.

Binding of the Reeds:
The Banishment of Topiltzin-Quetzalcoatl

> So it was that Topiltzin began to walk. Others say that he cast his mantle upon the sea, making a sign upon it with his hand, and, seating himself on the mantle, he then moved over the waters, never to be seen again.
> —FRAY DIEGO DURÁN, *Book of the Gods and Rites and the Ancient Calendar*

No longer the human
frame for world's sake
bones   the weight
and bend of sacrifice
my life for the sky's fall
between this long dying
flesh in war against flesh
to you I tell in vision
and glance once gone

toward death your morning
my hand to death the light

He writes:

      and the dead speak:
relentless horizon: unwilled harrow:

      spindle through the lake
that is wind
      & lineage:

solstice spilled
    on stone:

*Topiltzin drank the cursed white
octli from Titlacahuan's cup: with
sister Quetzalpetlatl he broke
chastity: covenant fallen: feather
diadem shattered*

In the cleft

    of leaf form
    & divide

the foretelling

white wing severed from wing's white
heron bled to blood the cane the reed

a distance without skies

He writes:

      the years
bound to renew the reeds:
through waters

waded: death a stone

    that rings at tide:

my own breathing has quieted
now this casting
from which we were chaste
until oaks give apples
until nightingales grow
beards like men
bitter the war bitter
my faith to be punished
my bitter unbinding
this casting toward east

He writes:

virtue of illusion: the corporeal
lost between sentence and sign:
        is the life without
memory flowing as cell: nerve

his face from his followers:
he flees Tollan: his body
he translates: to cacao tree:
to mesquite: flute singing leave-
taking:

          grating bone
against wind   this wind

through law   the *within* of such
things
          to such I cast you

          in shackle
          & saw

He writes:

turning as trace
in the body: a birth without
          time: without shadow:

a world weightless
      in indigence:

          without human blood
but other:
          in our name

leaf blight to leaf bitter
as master carved
to master to blind

our water stricken
when faith asked to punish
the pillar that is tendril
tendril that is torn

of this flesh where I till
this bitter unbound

He writes:
        the human body
hollow in altar: praisings

        of human threshing:
            leafless,

intentions white

at Tlapallan: a raft of
serpents:
casting his crafts into
Cozaapan:
river of jewels: he departs:
serpent into the risen dawn.

When waters return

recall
I am   jade of the shell wind
                this glass

when waters return

my grieving recall
this let in of
        light is
        never is to flowers

He writes:

        this earth: grass: harvest:
limestone:

        from spiralled shells, nakedness:

the earth's abeyance:

            testament of lightlessness:
                as the hand
            from his hand to water

Heredities
Letters of Relation

[a. or ad. OF. and F. *lettre*—L. *littera* a letter of the alphabet (pl. *litteræ* an epistle, written documents, records), also *litera* (in inscriptions *leitera*), of obscure origin.

—OED

Leitera—of origin, buttoned in black, translated
obscurity. God's missive given over to translation;
hence, loss. Or, *en arche en ho logos kai ho logos en pros
ton theon kai theos en ho logos.* The void littered across
parchment. The letter—the past come toward us
bearing utopian   promise, perfected negation.

First Letter

Your Majesties, so that you may know,

4
*No se llamé ni
examine el que no
estuviere
suficiétemente
testificado*
in the land of jaguar, heron,

fallow deer, hawk, and pigeon,
we colonized honor
—founding and settling

the royal crown, council and animosity:

at the hour of vespers,
when in view of stories
written according to wolf skin

featherwork, idol and slave,

hear this true account of Majesty and name.

i

In those parts

                that justice and reason
exchange for ruin and blood,

20
*Que siempre
declare el reo deba
xo delivramento
que tiene hecho.*

                we joined together as one mind

with gold that resembles shells.

                With four harpoons
                of white flint,

we discovered turtledoves
      in the open chest

                of diligence;
          we took out the heart and entrails,

burnt them in fifteen small gold bowls,
      fifteen small gold bells.

In 1519, Hernan Cortez sent five letters to
Emperor Charles V of Spain. Its paper a species of
wing without feather. The letter arrives as a
paper Christ extending cursive hands onto an
unspoken Lazarus, the past incarnated as word.
Cortez speaks of his "discovery" of New Eden.

ii

We gathered language

rendered in honey and beeswax
  from the beaks

54
Que se ha de hazer
vécié do el reo el
tormento.

                of peacocks,
        lined integrity with masonry

and mortar, gold and stone mosaic.

      At the hour of Mass,

        we grazed on justice,
    lips pierced with two needles of jade.

Translation of the letter:
> Cortez walks against a
> white field into irreducible
> otherness—a once barren valley
> grown over with pallid tapers.

Second Letter
Pertaining to the Discovery of Tenochtitlán

i

We sail the laws and beliefs

        of their idols, chambers garlanded

in feathers of little birds
        covered with pearl shells.

        Their past is a valley circular,
fertile in fruit and cotton,

        irrigated by channels carved
into the hands of slaves.

        Owls and sparrow hawks
          echo in the oratories,

        the reeds of the suns
            bound in their song.

ii. The Feast of the Innocents

Dressed in deerskin dyed white,

four hundred priests prostrated
themselves in the rooms

71
Los enfermos sean
curados, deseles
Confessor, si lo
pidre ren

of the hours, the walls tinted
the color of plum—in the center,

Montezuma ground green-

stone bones into flour.

A priest, with obsidian knife,
bled ruby jewelry from his penis

onto a mirror of sapphire.

The offering poured
over the lucent powder,

then molded into the shape
of a woman before being eaten.

iii

Within a pool of fresh water,
           unobserved, forty slave girls

             wearing muzzles of silk

           trade in salt and cane-birds,
             extracting providence

    from the lungs of kestrels—
       from each muzzled mouth hangs

     a latticework of canes,
           behind which the many gardens

      of fruit, sweet smelling flowers rise.

76
Como se há de dar
alimentos á la
mager, y hi jos del
reo.

In the valley of translation the hand is etymology
and reservoir; fingerprints—the whorls of language,
thought, and reality. Cortez's hands: twin rhetorics
washed in renunciation.

iv. The Kidnapping of Montezuma at the Palace of Quetzalcoatl

Four bridges carried by forty men

conquered Montezuma's faith—

the breaches in the wall

of prayer seized,

the calendar of suns civilized.

74
Como se ha de
hazer la
declaracion del
tiempo ǭ ha que el
reo coméco a ser
herege.

With spans of maize canes,
                his grace was stolen—

samples of its silver worn over

the face like a garment of water.

v. The Death of Montezuma

Taken to the roof of his resolution

that he might speak—

79
Declarase a los
reconcilia dos lo
que bá de cumplir,
y entreguerise al
Alcayde de la
carcel perpetua

Montezuma focused a golden arrow

on the principal temples;

he received a blow
on his head from a stone,
a censer opened

within the wound—the light,

whose name determined
he was, broke to pieces.

We built twelve brigantines

to cross the canal
hewn by the natives' tears.

Dona Marína said,

Between this brook in its fertility
and the part of the province

where fresh water passes to salt—

grief falls with tides,
a miter of gold

lost in the shallows.

[a. OF. *translation* (12th c. in Godef. *Compl.*), or ad. L. *translâtiôn-em* a transporting, translation, n. of action f. *translât-*,

I. 1.   a. Transference; removal or conveyance from one person, place, or condition
to another.
    b. *fig.* of non-material things.
    c. Removal from earth to heaven, *orig.* without death, as the translation of Enoch;
but in later use also said *fig.* of the death of the righteous.

—*OED*

             to translate: the transference of condition;
             translation of the letter: the materialization of
             origin without death. Cortez's slaughter: a
             harmony written in language—endless heavens
             brought to flesh.

Third Letter

God had given us

                       victory on the lake of canoes;

          our allies understood

               the entire land had retreated

              through fear into water,

17
Los Inquisidores no   *the music of idols*
traten có los reos   *buried in its body.*
fuera de sunegocio.

    i. Rebellion at Tenochtitlán

The natives ascended,

                rebelled; the enemy slew

                    forty Spaniards, a thousand

          of our Indian allies;

      those captured

              were bled with spines

           of obsidian, of maguey,

      skin flayed, heart torn

                from its ministration.

At dawn, we fell upon them,

              spearing, cutting countless

    numbers of men, women, and children;

         many pushed into waters

    where, tangled beneath bodies

           of brethren, they drowned.

Before the treasurer and contador,
                    their cause was pacified,

        the inevitability of their deaths

                        a gift of shields.

ii. The Massacre of La Noche Triste

Through the land which lies
in the domain of their courage,

32
Los Inquisidores
saqué las
publicaciones
firma das, os enala
das de sus nó bres,
os eñales

the enemy extracted

the lake's shores, the morning's

water their salvation.

At dawn, we showered them
with bolts from crossbows,

the writings of their kinships

burnt and torn down,
ashes spread across our foreheads.

iii. The Fall of Tenochtitlán

On the third day after Easter,
                    attacked with horsemen,
        sword, and lance,

      the city between birth
                                       81
                             Donde, y como se
                           han do renovar los
                           ambientos, lo que
           and baptism was taken—   *ha de contener el*
                           ambiento.

      pigeons, clay, amaranth,

               and uncut wood razed

        and burned—the earth

blinded into
fragments of naming.

Envoi

Leitera—of constant passage, concealment
ever arriving; the letter—the past incarnated
as trace, indivisible; the present, a mirror
ground to dust & swallowed.

That which is to man the self-existent, the highest being, to which he can conceive nothing higher—that is to him the Divine Being. How then should he inquire concerning this being, what he is in himself? If God were an object to the bird, he would be a winged being: the bird knows nothing higher, nothing more blissful, than the winged condition. How ludicrous would it be if this bird pronounced: to me God appears as a bird, but what he is in himself I know not.

—LUDWIG FEUERBACH

Articulations of Quetzalcoatl's Spine

Their god Quetzalcoatl . . . went to the heavens and said when he left that he would come again, and would bring his children . . .
—HERNANDO ALVARADO TEZOZOMOC, *Crónica Mexicana*

Ligaments Connecting the God's Spine to Creation

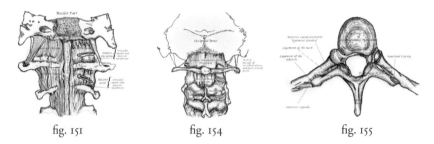

fig. 151   fig. 154   fig. 155

The *Anterior Occipito-atlantal Ligament* (fig. 153) is a broad membranous faith layer, composed of skirts of jade, paper diadem painted light blue. Here, providence supplies refuge. This ligament is in relation, in front, to the souls passing from their bodies; behind, with the time and longitudes of sweet ichor and dew.

The *Posterior Occipito-atlantal Ligament* (fig. 154) is a broad but thin membranous hope intimately blended with the manner of trees and fruits. It is in relation, behind, with those precepts presumed to lead toward perfection; in front, with the jaguar and eagle singled out for sacrifice.

The *Two Lateral Occipto-atlantal Ligaments* (fig. 153) are strong fibrous bands, offering maize and amaranth to the body whose praise is the human face. These ligaments are directed obliquely upward and inward, attached to the souls of infants transformed into hummingbirds; below, to the base of black hair attached to their mother, the first woman.

The *Two Capsular Ligaments* (fig. 155) surround the condyles of the occipital bone and connect them with the articular processes of the atlas; they consist of wept ashes, reeds of cane and water grasses; these enclose the narrow silence all hours become.

The Sternum of Our Lady of Guadalupe

"And of all those who love me, of those who cry to me, of those who search for me, of those who have confidence in me, in my Teocalli, I will listen to their cry, to their sadness, so as to curb all their different pains, their miseries and sorrows, to remedy and alleviate their sufferings . . . to realize what my compassionate, merciful gaze intends," she said to make known her precious will.
—ANTONIO VALERIANO, *Huei tlamahuiçoltica*

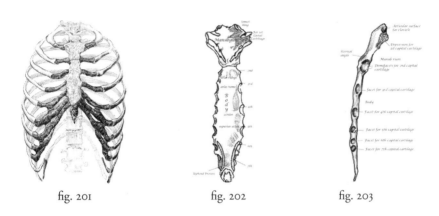

fig. 201   fig. 202   fig. 203

Her *Thorax* or *Chest* (fig. 201), an osseo-cartilaginous garden, contains the principal contemplations of the turquoise serpent, causality's unlimited sway. It is melody in shape, being a hymn of praise above and of marigold below.

Her *Sternum* (fig. 202), a flat, narrow island, situated in the marshes of the chest, consists of the seven caves of Aztlan. Convex in front, broad above, pure element where Heaven and the Day of Creation connect, her sternum points to a crown of twelve stars and thorn.

The *First Capilla of the Sternum* (fig. 203) is of moist light, spiced dew. Searching prayer from side to side, a broad canticle of flowers narrows below her faith. Each lateral border presents, at each angle, cavities pouring the vital fluids of history.

The *Second Capilla* (fig. 203), of piñon and discontinuity, is a union of fire, water, earth, and sky—the four violent passions language attempts to appease. The posterior surface, slightly concave, is marked by three authorities: form, measurement, and reason.

The *Third Capilla* (fig. 203) is a river of honey water among ceibas. Its anterior surface is temporally attached to the ceiba's branches; its posterior surface, with the lower levels of creation; from each angle hangs a necklace of human hand and heart—the law of origin, of muscle.

The Lady of Guadalupe's Dream and Jade Ruin

After Araki Yasusada's "Dream and Charcoal"

And she said: Does darkness list our erasures and become beautiful?

And she said: Those I love, I translate into advent and wild foxgrape,
      the blind staggers of water.

And then she said: The dead will return, narrow gates unlatched.

To which she replied: His body is air written between my hands.

Which is when she carved an arrow upon linden, leaf & chaff.

Which is when the butterflies hatched from her footprint.

Which was how she cut her fingers with seaweed and bitter jewel.

Which was when our martyr became the hour of unsung reeds.

III

Heredities (3) *Archetype*

The alley walls are lined with tapestries: of men tying the tongues of slaughtered bulls to their spears; of a young man dancing with a tuft of eagle plumes and a paper crown; of a man cutting his ear, holding a headless quail above him in offering.

Vendors sell pig heads, skinned chickens, chapolines. Like fingers, roasted red chiles hang from the walls. Alleys echo with men bargaining and smoking. In the doorways, women take the words of the curanderos, wet them with spit, and stick them to the foreheads of begging children.

The curanderos say the city is a tapestry—the Gods drive needles into the cloth of the earth to stitch the single pattern of fate; they barter their wares in the alleys of the heavens, peddling their woven worlds to less fortunate Gods. The Weaver Gods speculate that they themselves are merely images— heaven itself a tapestry hung from a wall that is a tapestry of itself.

Parable of the Pigeon

The pigeon followed her shadow to the shadow's nest.
She counted the twigs, divined the nature of figs & gnats.

Roosting in a fig tree before roasting
        in the hunter's hearth,

she begged the worm
        to turn the earth.

The earth turned its roots, eclipsed the sun,
while a pigeon wondered why figs must brown.

In the Year of the Jubilee

Through hibiscus,
      cereus, and hyphens,
   a woman ran,
crushing bulbs beneath her feet.

She plucked the first letters
      from their pollen,

swallowed sweet stem
      milk and soon

         after gave birth.

Ipalnemohua, angered,
      took acacia and grass,

the woman's body bound in ash.

                                         ☙

Abandoned beneath a green ceiba,
her infant among whitefly honey-

dew in a field of maize.

Quetzalcoatl,
dressed in locust
shell, ate through stalks
      of corn, sheltering

the child in jade husks,

bathed her
      within a horizon without light.

The child grew to womanhood,
black hair strung with shells whose ova
echoed watersong.

ã€€

What do you flee? the water asked.

Birth-blood, its running.

Bathe below my surface, the water spoke.

Stripping, she dived
into the stream. She swam

among silvery minnow.

The minnow questioned
the sky's permanence,
how one drinks air,

the textures of surface
where the heart hatches July and eglantine.

Rising from the water,
she dried herself
            on participles, laid herself
on the sand of the other shore.

She slept, she dreamt.

ã€€

She ran through fields
of desert lilies, plucked pollened sepals,
swallowed nations like names.

Then a crow stole the eggs

of a ruby-throated
hummingbird, taught the nestlings
to sing only at dusk.

The metallic
green crowned fledglings
settled on a firebrush branch,
magenta gorgets warbled
as they fed on fate
as if from nectar.

In the crow nest,
among the broken
spotted shells—dry leaves

of the rosita de cacao, white
leavings, a tear in silence,
a blue button.

&

She rode the curved
plates of an armadillo

through gardens of amaranth,

lived in the shell of a snail,
grass as bedding, singing,

con el oido lleno de flores recien cortadas
con la lengua llena de amor y de agonia.

A butcher offered her
        a place to sleep

                among forked tongs,

            knives, hanging tripe,
        head pillowed against the womb
                    of a heifer.

                        ❧

Brushing sand from her black hair,
        she rose. The sand kept
            the gulf her body left,
                        pooling tears into the shallows.

Between her middle and index fingers,
a caterpillar cocooned in prayer.

            She pursed her lips,
            watched white spotted wings
            ringed in black

            pull from webbed chrysalis.

She fed the fritillary passion
        fruit and context.

                        ❧

She walked naked, barefoot
toward a solitary hacienda.
A man approached with a twig basket
      in a mantle of distance
        torn from its sky.

He handed her this name.

She offered the shell
      of an uncoiled snail.

The Quietest Heaven

Mama let me walk on the floor
without shoes. She let me walk

without shoes today, she smiles.
I sit, listen to my mother

walk barefoot through her
unanchored memory—

a blanched nightgown
whispering against tile,

leaves blowing on grass.

White Song

She leans her head into the white
sheets. sheets a cruel sweetness:
her eyes doe blind: she prays
lilac   in   hand.   counting
calyx to stamen. stamen to leaf:
her   faith   is   of   the   body:
what   is   the   body   in   the   bed:
lilac   and   grace.
in   a   vase   lilacs   push   thin
weight   into   white.
water   turned   milk
coursing   through   cut   stem:
water-pale   white   song: yes.
grandmother   in   sheets: no:
grandmother is a photo of white
sheets: she   is   beside   a   vase
of   lilacs: yes: leaf-blind: no:
not yet: she bakes bruised apples
sweet   with   sugar.   cinnamon.
brings the shriveled sweet things
on a plate. stems warm. a plate
of stems: no: the plate was from
before. a photo is the word for
before: the   distance   the   body
reaches   for   essence   in   image:
grandmother is the word for
white image and apples. the word
is   stem   and   apples   falling.
fall speech fall: she is speech-
fallen: grandmother quilts lilacs
on a sheet: quilts lilacs on speech.
a   daffodil   in   her   hair   as
needle and thread. thread-speech.
she threads her white: white her
wreath   of   speechless   lilac   and
keep. grandmother leans her head

into the white. sheets a cruel
sweetness. her mouth is deathless
calyx to stamen. stamen to leaf:
is deathless is. her leaf sings.
deathless is. mouth waterpale.
watersong   pale   white.

Portrait of an Iris

You are   porcelain pretty one   *little word cupshaped*   tracing seasons still holding to
branches   when the eye is an hour in autumn   beneath rimmed tuning

the iris   focuses its petals   in the reproduction of forms   air flowering
into light what light will acknowledge   scattering   what Gods   reside in promise

you are a human event   growth   air   hibiscus   artery
                seabird   shellfish   unstruck song   the raw materials necessary to creation

in you   the enduring   desire to shape in hierarchy   the intimate authority
                of paradise   you must step away from this   to know this earth

Meister Eckhart's Sermon on Flowers and the Philosopher's Reply

A hollowed singularity exists in flowers
like pathos in a dandelion:
an eddy of fate, degreeless,

silvering through memory.
A scabbed consonant departing
the sentence: locust petal, bromeliad,

a surfacing shame, lightless, beyond hearing.
Solitary, the clock circumvents sound
and a horse importunes

a wasp bowing before significance.

&

It is in fact doubtless a wasp bows before significance
degreeless in a dandelion.

It also stands to reason that, in a clock, locusts circumvent memory
in order to depart through fate.

And anyone can see that singularity exists lightless
like an eddy of pathos surfacing beyond hearing.

In conclusion, however solitary
(and you know this as well as I),

a consonant will always
depart the sentence before shamed by a horse.

Atopos

Atopos: the loved being is recognized by the amorous subject as atopos . . . i.e. unclassifiable, of a ceaselessly unforeseen originality.
—ROLAND BARTHES, *A Lover's Discourse*

[1] *Dimly We Apprehend the Double Movement: Self to the Other, I to Thou*

Owing to eyelids, I drew an equator through our desire to section the truths we never cared to recognize. I said, The Northern Hemisphere is the caress of your neck. You said, Skin is the boundary relating origin to noun. I gave you a gift of orchids with stigmas patterned purple, pollen sacs dusted white. You tell me my tongue is the latitude of constant vanishing.

[2] *Dialogue Is the Connect between Violent Compassion and Understanding*

You told me my tongue is the latitude of constant vanishing. I said, I rush through the dispersed body of the sky. Rain, you said, is the moment when commas can no longer hold their clauses. You place a jar of dead butterflies before you. You said, Open the aorta to allow the human impulse to imagine. My finger rubs against your language where the snowfield is crisp against the skin.

[3] *Language Is Drawn through the Faith the Heart Denies*

Where the snowfield is crisp against the skin, forget the lack the body carries. You said, Lift the silk water on your tongue; there will be light; there will be the leaf when autumn has stripped the preposition bare. I watch a caterpillar pull itself across an atrophied wing. I said, There is no horizon in this, only an aperture through which human desire comes to know itself as verb, flux, and commencement. You said, The skin will volta between histories.

[4] *To Name Is to Reduce the Amorous Subject to an Object*

You said, The skin is pallid beneath the noun. I said, Confidence is the faith in the reciprocity of acting and being. You take my name gently in your hands and unpeel: *Michael, My, Call, I, cull, Miguel, Me, cell, Mi, compel, My comb, womb, wound, sought, caught, capture, conceal, leap, lunge, lose, confuse, con, call, saw, me, Michael.* You discard these peelings like callused skin.

[5] *Undo the Name to Undo the Ego*

I said, Light peels from the sky like callused skin. You said, The last name
must be sung: *Martinez, mar, teen, is, mart, I, nest, mar, I, nest, which is to
say, To nest is to is to I to nest to mar the I.* The words unfold from your body.
I winter there from noun to verb beneath your maiden name.

[6] *To Come to Love: Self-contradict into Ecstasies*

I wintered there from noun to verb beneath your maiden name. I said, The Southern Hemisphere is the clean bruise of the hours. I said, Open the closure. You said, Break the window, let the wind cool the subjunctive: we will merge in the solstice of the noun. You hold an orchid in your hand. A strand of blonde hair falls to the table.

I said, The only connect is cellular habit; arteries driving the body toward extremity's definite form.

You say, Have faith in the interval, the human and the name, lay the orchid among the hair.

Heredities (4) *Amma*

Maria Jesus y Maria Jesus y Marie,
the voyages of names, black sails inked with their dead,

the *No* consecrated on my mother's hand:
Maria Jesus y Maria Jesus y Marie

a thousand serpents crawl along the waves
breaching shore for its salt.

Near ourselves, we return:
Mother, crown where the eye-

      lash has fallen   through you:
      eat the carcass, eat morning's edge;

      at the ends,   its past—
      where forms of an impossible prison

mark the flesh, where salt is
and Voice walks the garden, tolling

those destined for the plague, to the plague
those destined for captivity, to captivity
those destined for the sword, to the sword;

for those plagued, for those
captive, for those with sword

      drink Mother, drink:

the native land language is
is traced eyeless
           in the heart,
           the law steers you

seasoned with marrow,
tolling the thickness of images.

ii

I have held the palm branch,
I have seen the wheels jeweled
      in crest
      & swallow:

Mother, you will pass & I will pass with you
into the tabernacle to leave
peerless architecture
the heirs   the hands
      of weeds

we will boil nostalgia's carrion
tongue wish taproot
    sobre nuestras cabezas en llamas

      cartilage
& sound's nest steamed to stew

we will pour over our hands
these clarities into dirt

& blossom mesquite's clustered amber

      flowers   the end
          -law of maidens sung by feasting bees:

      Maria y Maria y Maria y Maria

      in the hive, the honey will host

a name's leprosy,   our pores' visible ruin.

We will drum the hive & the hive will drum our flesh,
crawling into our swallowing mouths, belly swarmed pregnant,
our nakedness blistered beneath
                              birth's stinging harps.

iii

Mother,

        you will pass
        with you: in me,

        the name will be
        no cradle to nurse.

Notes

This heritage of identifications poses challenges because taking oneself as part
of the avant-garde tempts writers to dismiss major aspects of their heritage—and, hence,
to ignore other, less radical ways of characterizing contemporaneity.

—CHARLES ALTIERI, *Avant-Garde or Arrière-Garde in Recent American Poetry*

འ

The epigraph by Octavio Paz at the beginning of the book is from the chapter
entitled "The Other Shore" in *The Bow and the Lyre*.

"Heredities: *Etymology*": A *curandera* is a healer who uses herbs, spiritualism, and
other means to heal and divine.

"Heredities: *Corporeity*": The word *rebisabuelo* translates to "great-great-
grandfather." A *partera* is a curandera who specializes as a midwife.

"Water Poppies Open as the Mouth": The epigraph and the italicized phrases are
from Maurice Merleau-Ponty's *Phenomenology of Perception*.

"Binding of the Reeds: The Banishment of Topiltzin-Quetzalcoatl": The Meso-
American myth of Topiltzin-Quetzalcoatl, the Lord of Tollan, varies from region
to region. H. B. Nicholson details hundreds of versions of this myth in his book
Topiltzin-Quetzalcoatl: The Once and Future Lord of the Toltecs (Boulder: Univer-
sity Press of Colorado, 2001). One version has the priest Quetzalcoatl stopping
human sacrifice in Toltec culture and establishing the worship of the deity
Quetzalcoatl through the burning of butterflies, snakes, and herbs. The priest
Quetzalcoatl was rumored to have "cultured" the Toltecs, bringing knowledge
of music, the arts, and, most importantly, writing. He was also rumored to have
been light-skinned and bearded. Quetzalcoatl led a life of chastity, refraining
from liquor and sex, eating only simple food, wearing simple dress.

    The priest Titlacahuan was supposedly the god Tezcatlipoca. In the narra-
tive, when Quetzalcoatl forbade human sacrifice (the worship of Tezcatlipoca
demanded human sacrifice) Titlacahuan in revenge drugged Quetzalcoatl with
white octli, an intoxicating liquor. In one version of the myth, Quetzalcoatl

raped his sister Quetzalpetlatl while he was drugged; the next morning, after recovering, Quetzalcoatl wore an elaborate mask of feathers and jade to hide his shame. Quetzalcoatl either fled Tollan or was banished by his followers. On his journey from Tollan he transformed himself into various objects, including a cocoa tree; wherever he traveled he brought "culture" to the peoples.

Upon arriving at the eastern shore of present-day Mexico, Quetzalcoatl built a craft of serpents to sail over the ocean. Burning in the flames of a bonfire built on the boat, Quetzalcoatl rose to become the morning star. (The final image is an echo of the Mexica creation myth in which Quetzalcoatl sacrifices himself in fire to create time, igniting the sun.) Depending on the myth, Quetzalcoatl, while burning, either cursed the Meso-Americans and prophesied their destruction by the arrival of the Spanish, or prophesied his return and his redemption of Meso-America from the clutches of a future evil. The myths both affirm and contradict each other in this complicated and tragic narrative.

The phrase "death that rings at tide" is from my collaboration with poets Anne Heide and James Belflower.

"Heredities: Letters of Relation": The lyrical sections of this sequence are wholly composed of language from Hernan Cortez's *Letters from Mexico* (New York: Grossman, 1971), translations by A. R. Pagden of Cortez's five letters sent during the conquest. The italicized sidenotes are from Bishop Tomas Torquemada's *Compilacio De Las Instrucciones Del Oficio De La Santa Inquisicion*. Published in 1667, the text is a compilation of all the edicts Bishop Torquemada published on how to prosecute the Spanish Inquisition. There are two known versions of this vellum text, one located in a museum in Spain, the other at the Library of Congress. I have kept all idiosyncrasies of the original text intact.

The quotation on page 45 is from Ludwig Feuerbach's *The Essence of Christianity*.

Images in "Articulations of Quetzalcoatl's Spine" and "The Sternum of Our Lady of Guadalupe" are ink on paper, based on *Gray's Anatomy*, drawn by J. Michael Martinez.

Thanks to Matthew Ross Thomas for his pencil and ink art of Guadalupe's Ribcage.

"Our Lady of Guadalupe's Dream and Jade Ruin" is after Araki Yasusada's poem "Dream and Charcoal." Araki Yasusada is purportedly a survivor of Hiroshima. But after publication and accolades for his book, sources revealed he never existed. Araki Yasusada is the pseudonym of a still unknown author.

"In the Year of the Jubilee": Ipalnemohua is one of the names of the dual-god Ometéotl, the Lord and Lady of Duality. Ipalnemohua translates to "giver of life." In *Aztec Thought and Culture: A Study of the Ancient Nahuatl Mind* (Norman: University of Oklahoma Press, 1990), Miguel León-Portilla writes: "Recognizing that he had his roots in the mysterious duality of the Divine, Nahuatl man acknowledged Ometéotl's transcendency by declaring that he was invisible like the night and intangible like the wind. Feeling all this, the pre-Columbian thinker asked himself if he would someday live in the presence of the Giver of Life, in her dwelling place, from which the 'flowers and songs' came." Quetzalcoatl, revered in contemporary Chicano culture, translates to "the serpent with plumes of the quetzal" (the *quetzal* is an iridescent green bird of the tropical jungles); Quetzalcoatl is, in myth, father of the sun and also the god who brought arts and culture to Meso-Americans. The italicized text in Spanish is from Federico García Lorca's poem "Gacel X: De la huida" ("Ghazal of the Flight").

"Portrait of an Iris": The italicized phrases are from Alice Notley's poem "Alma," in her book of the same name.

"Heredities: Amma": The italicized Spanish phrase is from Octavio Paz's poem "El Mismo Tiempo" ("Identical Time").

❧

You said, The infinite is the origin you foster.
I said, History gathers in the name we never are.

❧